Baxter's journey from self-doubt to self-acceptance is truly heart-touching! This charming story reminds us that being true to ourselves is not only the key to finding where we truly belong, but also the most powerful door opener and strength we all have!

— **Carolina López Saglietti,**
Global Inter-Generational Transformation Leader,
Bestselling Author of *How I Became a Superhero,*
Founder of SuperHero Programs and the Queen Method

Sherry Dunn has once again captured the hearts of young readers with *Baxter and the Power of Mud*. This touching tale of self-acceptance and resilience, told through the eyes of an endearing shelter dog, is a must-read for children and animal lovers alike. A beautifully written story with a powerful message!

— Vladimira Kuna, Belief & New Mind Leader,
Award-Winning International Bestselling Author,
Host at Faith Building Podcast

Baxter is a dog that is always full of energy and mischief. Yet he wants so desperately to be adopted by a human that he goes through great lengths with the help of his friends to change his appearance and personality. But he discovers in the end that being himself is what really matters most. Baxter and the Power of Mud will definitely be one of those books your child will want to read more than once.

— Louise Malecha, International Bestselling Author of
Going to Papa and Nana's Farm and *Ginger's Big Day*

Baxter and the Power of Mud is a heartfelt story that highlights the journey of shelter pets and the magic of finding the perfect match. Baxter's adventure is a touching reminder that our quirks make us special—and sometimes, a little mud is just what's needed to bring people (and pups!) together.

— Judy O'Beirn, Founder and President of Hasmark Publishing International

This book is such a fun read with bright, lively illustrations and an equally engaging plot and characters. I absolutely love the encouraging message behind it. You're in store for a great read with this one!

— Eugenie Gloria Wong, Award-Winning and International Bestselling Author of *Penny's Day on the Farm*

Jasmine's Paws & Tales Series

Baxter and the Power of Mud

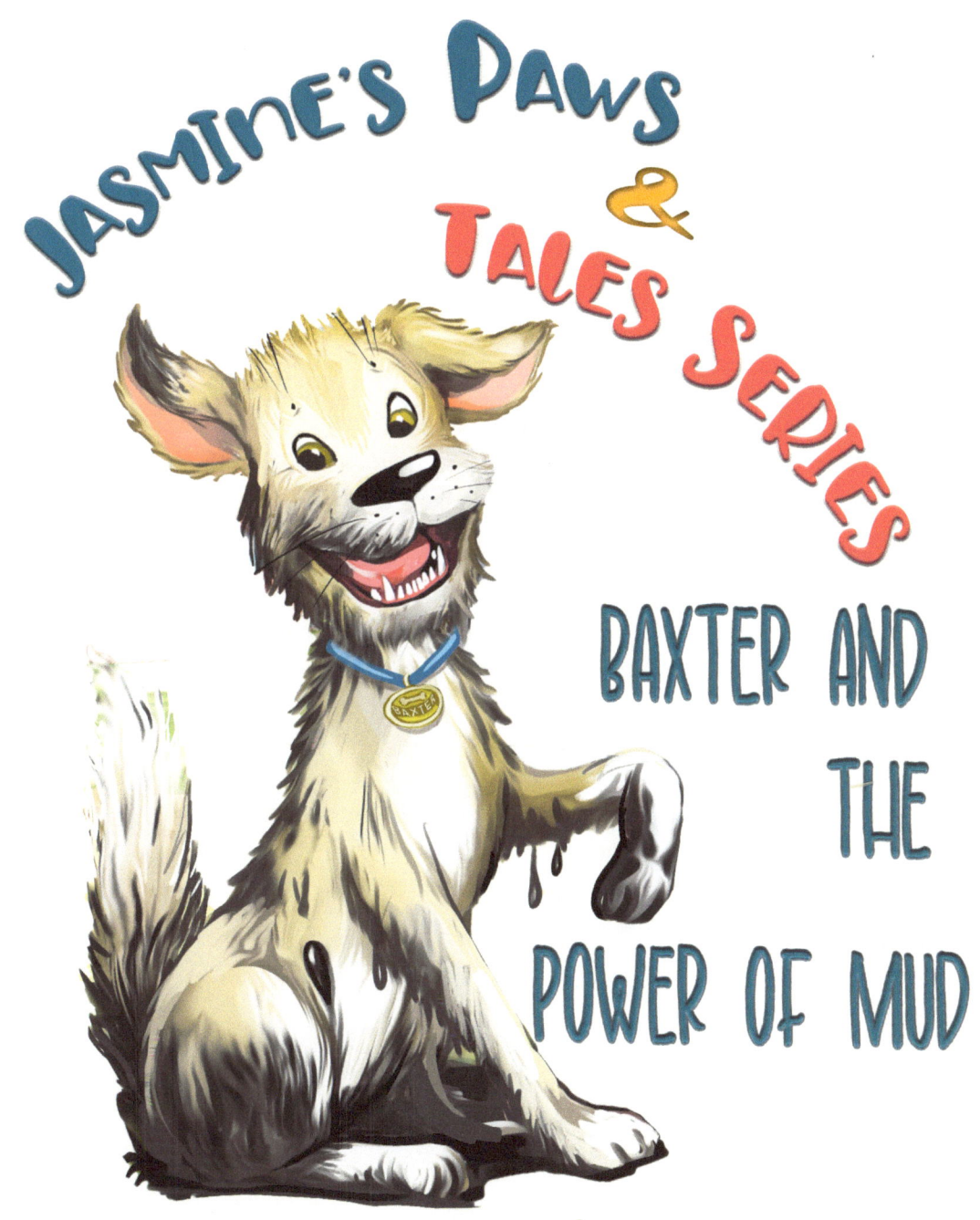

BOOK #1 IN THE JASMINE'S PAWS & TAILS SERIES

Written By
Sherry Dunn

Illustrated By
Nino Aptsiauri

Published by
Hasmark Publishing International
www.hasmarkpublishing.com

Copyright © 2025 Sherry Dunn

First Edition

No part of this book may be reproduced or transmitted in any form or by any means, electronic or mechanical, including photocopying, recording or by any information storage and retrieval system, without written permission from the author, except for the inclusion of brief quotations in a review.

Disclaimer

This book is designed to provide information and motivation to our readers. It is sold with the understanding that the publisher is not engaged to render any type of psychological, legal, or any other kind of professional advice. The content of each article is the sole expression and opinion of its author, and not necessarily that of the publisher. No warranties or guarantees are expressed or implied by the publisher's choice to include any of the content in this volume. Neither the publisher nor the individual author(s) shall be liable for any physical, psychological, emotional, financial, or commercial damages, including, but not limited to, special, incidental, consequential or other damages. Our views and rights are the same: You are responsible for your own choices, actions, and results.

Permission should be addressed in writing to Sherry Dunn at sherry@sherrydunn.com.

Editor: Karen Cioffi-Ventrice [kcioffiventrice@gmail.com]
Cover Design: Anne Karklins [anne@hasmarkpublishing.com]
Interior Layout: Amit Dey [amit@hasmarkpublishing.com]
Illustrator: Nino Aptsiauri [artninka@gmail.com]

ISBN 13: 978-1-77482-311-8
ISBN 10: 1-77482-311-X

Dedication

I dedicate this book to Jasmine,
my muse and the heart behind
the **Maddie and Jasmine series,**
as well as the new adventures in
Jasmine's Paws & Tales Series.
You waited patiently at the animal shelter
for three long years until we found each other.
Your unwavering spirit inspires me every day.

"Splash. Splash. Splash."

Baxter's tail creates big ripples as he paddles. Frothy waves spill over the sides of the kiddie pool. He's at it again.

"Woof. Woof. Woof!"

Baxter bites at the waves.

"Snort. Snort. Snort."

Baxter shakes his head to get a snot bubble off his nose.

Baxter spots a pile of dead leaves.

"Hey, Baxter!" shouts Jasmine. "I thought I'd find you near the pool."

"Jasmine!" Baxter's tail wags so much he nearly falls over. "Why are you here?" A lump forms in his throat. "Did your human, Maddie, bring you back?"

"Nope," purrs Jasmine. "She volunteers here now, and I come with her. What about you?"

Today is my 999th day at the shelter. Nobody wants to adopt me," Baxter sighs. "If I were softer or smaller, maybe someone would want me. I usually smell like a wet dog because I love the kiddie pool.

"The shelter always features me in adoption events. They say I'm friendly and love water. Tomorrow is another adoption day. I need to look better."

"You're already quite the looker," says Jasmine. "Let's step it up a notch. Who can join our little makeover squad?"

"Lucky's here! She'll help," barked Baxter.
"She's a big-time napper, but she'd lend a paw.
OH, OH, OH, I can't forget Rory. Always looks sharp!
Bet he's got grooming tips up his furry sleeve!"

Jasmine sees Lucky waddling around a corner.

"What's up?" panted Lucky. "Jasmine, did Maddie bring you back?"

"No," says Jasmine. "I'm here to help out."

"What's going on?" asks Rory as he greets the group with a slow wag of his bushy tail. Rory quietly asks Lucky and Baxter, "Did Maddie bring her back?"

"Nope," says Baxter. "She's good. We'll see a lot more of Jasmine around here."

"Let's get started," yells Baxter. "I need a makeover!"

"I got this," says Rory.

Rory, the Doodle, gently and patiently brushes Baxter's tangled fur. "Lots of twigs and leaves falling out," says Rory.

"I'll be in charge of the warm, bubble bath," says Lucky. She scrubs Baxter clean, using her paws to get all the hard-to-reach spots.

Once Baxter is clean, Jasmine oversees the finer details with her perfect grooming habits and her well-known golden paw. She fluffs Baxter's fur. She cleans his face and ears and checks for remaining dirt.

By the end of their grooming session, Baxter looks spotless.

"Here, Baxter," meows Jasmine. "How about this blue collar?"

Barks and howls of approval ring throughout the kennel.

"I think he's ready for tomorrow's adoption event," says Jasmine. "Remember! Stay clean!"

The shelter buzzes with activity on the day of the event.

A young couple walks into the shelter, their hiker shoes scuffle against the floor.

"Baxter sounds perfect for our weekend hikes," the man says as he reads Baxter's story. 'Wild and scruffy!'

But instead of 'wild and scruffy',
Baxter stands tall, shows a regal presence, and is
immaculately groomed. He sits patiently and looks
every bit the dignified dog.

"I don't think Baxter is the right fit for us," says the woman. "We're active hikers and need a dog who enjoys the outdoors and isn't afraid of a little mud. Baxter seems too neat, tidy, and quiet for our lifestyle."

"Oh no, not again," Baxter whimpers.

"Oh yeah? Watch this!" Baxter springs into action. His paws thud against the floor as he runs toward the door. His tail wags fast and uncontrollable, ready to enjoy the great outdoors.

He heads to the kiddie pool.

"Woohoo!" He spots his muddy paradise and makes a beeline for it.

Baxter's eyes are wide, and his tongue hangs to the side. He rolls and rolls. His coat is now dirt and crud.

Baxter gallops over to the couple and shakes.

Water and mud fly everywhere.

Lucky's paws cover her eyes.
Jasmine's tail twitches. Rory yells,
"You're throwing mud all over those people!"

The young couple look at each other, chuckle at the mud-coated Baxter, and head to the front desk laughing.

A chunk of grass falls from the woman's glasses.

About the Author

Children's author and animal rescue advocate, Sherry Dunn discovered her passion writing for children after a career in the Human Resources field. She is an avid reader, and writing seemed to follow naturally.

She is a three-time International Best-Selling Author, a three-time recipient of the Gold Mom's Choice Award, a Hasmark International Publishing 2023 Award of Excellence Recipient, and a Hasmark International Publishing 2024 Award of Excellence in the Children's Books category recipient.

Sherry is the catalyst behind the **Kids to Kitties Reading Program** at the Humane Society of St. Lucie County in Port St. Lucie, Florida. This program creates a mutually beneficial experience for students, ages 6-15, looking to enhance their reading skills and for shy, anxious shelter cats in need of comfort and companionship.

Sherry is a Member of the Association of Professional Humane Educators (Empathy through Education). She is also a member of the Society of Children's Book Writers and Illustrators, Children's Book Insider, and the Institute of Children's Literature. Learn more about Sherry at www.sherrydunn.com.

Sherry lives on Florida's beautiful Treasure Coast with her seventh rescue cat, Jasmine.

When she's not writing, Sherry likes to read, play the piano, paint in watercolor, and work with local art groups and local animal shelters.

Learn more about Sherry at www.sherrydunn.com.

For more info about Sherry

Social Media Networks/Handles:
- Facebook: https://www.facebook.com/sherry.dunn.3158/
- Instagram: maddieandjasmine
- Linkedin: https://www.linkedin.com/in/sheryl-dunn-a4234874
- Beekonnected: Sherrydunn
- Sherry Dunn PawsInPrint, LLC

Website: http://sherrydunn.com
Email: sherry@sherrydunn.com

Become a Guest Blogger

Sherry Dunn's mission is to share the stories of shelter pets and help them find their forever homes.

Discover heartwarming tales in Sherry's latest blogs featuring Animal Adoption Stories, shining a spotlight on exceptional Animal Shelters, offering insightful tips in the Tail Talk Central, and providing engaging reviews of delightful Picture Books

Interested in Being a Guest Blogger?

For every guest post accepted and published to Sherry's blog, she will donate $100 to the author's favorite animal shelter/rescue (provided it is a no-kill facility)!

For submissions guidelines visit: https://sherrydunnbooks.com/guest-bloggers

To submit your submissions (and photos) please email sherry@sherrydunn.com.

Sherry Dunn

ANIMAL RESCUE ADVOCATE, AUTHOR, SPEAKER

The MADDIE AND JASMINE Series

Discover the profound impact of friendship and the transformative power of pet companionship.

Available on Amazon NOW!

Maddie and Jasmine, an **International Bestselling** series by **Award-Winning** author **Sherry Dunn**, serves as a poignant narrative of self-discovery, resilience against bullying, and embracing individuality. With themes of compassion towards animals and the importance of adoption from shelters, these heartwarming tales inspire readers to cherish differences and extend kindness to all beings.

From their initial encounter in book 1, to the eagerly anticipated conclusion in book 3, **Maddie and Jasmine** exemplify the enduring bonds of friendship and the universal need for acceptance, making it a captivating read for all ages.

Upcoming Books

Join Jasmine's many shelter & rescue animal friends in their own exciting adventures in a new series!

For more info on these and upcoming books, visit https://sherrydunn.com